MW00453263

OTHER WORLDS

PITT POETRY SERIES

Ed Ochester, Editor

OTHER WORLDS

ALBERT GOLDBARTH

UNIVERSITY OF PITTSBURGH PRESS

Published by the University of Pittsburgh Press, Pittsburgh, Pa., 15260
Copyright © 2021, Albert Goldbarth
All rights reserved
Manufactured in the United States of America
Printed on acid-free paper
10 9 8 7 6 5 4 3 2 1

ISBN 13: 978-0-8229-6669-2
ISBN 10: 0-8229-6669-7

Cover art: Painting by Skyler Lovelace
Cover design: Melissa Dias-Mandoly

for Skyler

Loving her was his success.

—Michael Malone, *Dingley Falls*

A chord in the music just then woke a thin shivering wire of sound at the back of my brain, and for an instant the barrier between this world and the worlds outside was as thin as air.

—Henry Kuttner

At the margins of any tale there are lives that come into it for only a moment. Or, put another way, there are those who run quickly through a story and then out, along their paths. For these figures, living their own sagas, the tale they intersect is the peripheral thing. A moment in the drama of their own living and dying.

—Guy Gavriel Kay

CONTENTS

Mourn & Pre-Mourn

Touching on Recent American History

Amazing Stories

Stories

OTHER WORLDS

Mourn & Pre-Mourn

Memory is the only afterlife I can understand.

—Lisel Mueller

Last Song

I choose the other way,
with heels dug in.
I vote for screaming

yearningly. For heading to the afterlife
against the grain of this one. For a slowing down
to the pace of a person too absorbed
in the glory and grit
to work up any hurry for departing it.
I choose greedily looking backward
at each freestone peach and grubby radiator cap,
each watermelon seed and hypodermic needle,
jonquil, castanet, railroad spike. And even so,
by now—I'm seventy-three—I've seen enough

to know that there are ample reasons
of psychology and circumstance for a quiet,
accepting, meltaway transition
from this plane of muscle and capillary
and Shakespeare's plays and Afro-plaited hair.
I choose the other way,

remembering the adamant drag
of Rembrandt's burin over the resistant surface,
bringing out a crown of light
over Jesus's head, as well as the granary shadows
rats make more rats in.
He was true to these: precise, and with integrity.
With ardor.
I want to snag in the folds like a burr.
I want to remora
onto the bellyflesh of creation.
Every anther. Every pollen grain, that under

magnification resembles the Taj Mahal.
And the Taj Mahal. The grouting—not much different
from yours or mine—that's necessary even in
the Taj Mahal. If I must go, I want my teethmarks

on the inner velvet nap of nearby tree bark, saying
I went, but in a frenzy of refusal. Let me be a squatter
standing with a shotgun in the doorway labeled Breath.
I want to be a cult—if only a cult of only me—
that won't vacate the compound. I choose to be stubborn,
I want to be full-on jackass stubborn over Einstein's
spidery scrimmage of equations, over the gelid mass
of a fresh lung in the transplant tray, I choose to be a miser
of jewels and breasts, of sewage treatment plants.
An inch cube of beryllium. A scimitar hilt.
An alligator pear.
The *no* of Rosa Parks, on loan to me.
I want to be witnessed

floating above the hospital bed, still tethered
by the paying-out tube of a catheter

the way the astronaut's corded
to the mother ship on a space walk.
I want to be witnessed,
witnessed rising to the ceiling
still attached by that stem.
I want to be unwilling.

Praxilla (fifth century B. C.)

> His love of simple things was not always understood. For example, he "mentioned cucumbers along with the sun and the moon."
>
> —Richard Lattimore

The news tonight: a car on fire,
so frighteningly ugly-bright
against the lightless street,
its orange daggerflower flames
might be a test from the minions of Hell itself
to see if a fuller invasion
of the surface world is feasible. Given the rest
of the news, the answer is yes. The powers
of legitimate unrest and the powers of brute
and mindless violence have become
—without either side seeking this out—the two
flanks of a single nightmare army on the move.
There will be more of cars
as makeshift bombs, and more of people
behind the wheel as fuses.
Is it wrong, right now, to want to write a poem

in which the sunlight slices through the blinds
of the bedroom window, muted
by the trees to a shade of apricot, and
burnishes my wife's already coppery hair
as she sleeps? Is it wrong to remember
we went to the zoo this week, and when
she took my hand between the rhino
and the ocelot, my palm
was the calmest, maybe the happiest,
patch of animal life for a mile around?
The deaths from COVID . . .
and the deaths in the streets . . .

is it wrong to say I don't want to die
as much as anybody has ever not wanted to die

in a world of garden leaves
that follow the arc of the sun in the sky
like an audience that follows a celebrity
across the stage; and books that I treasure;
and friends that I treasure;
and carmelizing onions; and those bags
of mini-cucumbers I buy at Trader Joe's
that have come from Canada
to lay their benediction on my tongue.

Summer, 2020
Wichita, Kansas

Duet

in memoriam, Michael Cissell

The Russian experiment—from the 1950s—
in which the baby rabbits aboard a submarine
were killed—their necks were snapped—
and in a cage in a lab in Leningrad,
that same second, the mother rabbit shrieked.

How subtle, how ethereally silken, we've learned
to make that experiment. Chinese scientists
have split apart pairs of photons,
one of them "teleported up to a satellite
orbiting 300 miles overhead," and yet "remaining
entangled with its partner on Earth."
I don't know how they recognize "entanglement"
on that level—it isn't lovers' legs
in bed, after all—but I trust their wacko-physics expertise.

The twin who died of a heart attack
in Oakland, California, as his sister
awoke in a chilly slip of sweat
in Haven, Connecticut.
The infant who wakes with a hungry cry
and, out in the car in the driveway, the mother
—although she can't hear him, not literally—
can feel the pearlescent petals begin
to blossom out of her nipples.

If we could beam a consciousness
to Mars, would it scream

from a nightmare in the subconscious
we kept back on Earth?

Would the brain still thrill in pleasure,
in a nutrient solution rocketing out of the solar system,
when the body of its entanglement
was sexually aroused in Dayton, Ohio?

My friend Michael loves to play
acoustic guitar (his son's named Guthrie
after Woody). He does a soulful
"Saint James Infirmary." But he also has
some electric whooziewhatsis machine

that records him, then replays it in a loop,
so he can accompany himself,
can be two Michaels, a duet—but
from a single egg.
If I weren't here in his living room watching,
making him self-conscious, I think
he'd be rocking out ecstatically.

"Ecstasy"—that is, "out of one's own body,"
"to be beside one's self."

Reshelving

What is it, with these novels?
People are always dying. Even
—often especially—the people
I've come to like. The unwed mother,
shamed by her own family for that single
consequential act of careless love, who
(over chapters of complicated narrative engine-rev:
the opioids; the asthma; her job defined by wiping
withered-up Assisted Living asses) rises
into the echelons of heroism: but dies
three-fourths of the way to the final page.
The Buddhist warrior: the same. His nights
excruciating over ideas of justice
in an unjust world, parsing "duty,"
parsing the weights of "necessity" versus "decency"
that he sets down in the moonlight
on the balance-pans of his conscience—this
won't save him when the plot requires his being
offered up. And some novels are *nowhere* near
that chintzy; their dead get scattered throughout
prodigiously, as if some great piñata of mortality
were struck, and cracked, and its contents
unloosed: gang war, gulag, killing field,
the Biblical Flood, the podcast on Ebola.
It's a simple question flippered like a pinball
through my head tonight—simplistic,
even—but still worth sharing,
knowing as I do that TL's cousin OD'd
yesterday (it was heroin); and the cancer
claimed another unit in W's
condominium of a spine, and soon will own it
in entirety; and hovering over these two,
from a month ago: P's suicide, P's (she was

a physician) self-prescribed and pill-by-pill
renunciation of the world.
And Michael—when his wallet was lifted
out of his unlocked car, within an hour "he"
was spreeing through the nearest WalMart, loading up
from every aisle; one year later real-Michael
suffered a cardiac arrest and never recovered;
maybe it's small of me, but he was my friend,
and my wish is that fake-Michael became
so quantumly entangled with the original, he
fell over, in the same sick sweat, the same time.
With this roll call out of "real life," who needs,
as a mnemonic, some skeletal tug at the sleeve,
these books wherein the cadavers are being positioned
onto their stone slabs in an ancient Egyptian mortuary,
and—the 1950s—a body is lifted out of its minimalist
chalk outline as a conveyance the cops
so charmingly call "the meat wagon" roars to the curb.
Some nights my easy question haunts me, haunts me
equally under the mystery text
the stars code into the sky, or driving diminished
beside the eerily lit-up dynamos of the power company
talking to each other with inhuman bolts of charge.
These novels. . . .Why do we call them "fiction"?
They're "biography" told through identity theft.

Atlanta, 1899

After Sam Hose, a black farmer, was lynched, he was dismembered, and
barbequed, and his body parts were sold as souvenirs. W. E. B. Du Bois saw
his knuckles displayed in a store window.

—as reported in Jill Lepore's *These Truths*

If I were stronger right now I'd research
more. What he did; what he was said
to have done; the pants
he wore (that he shit, as the animal
hiding in his eyes took over and "terror"
wasn't merely a word but a stink in the air,
a slobber that predates language); and also
what animals the crowd became as his skin
began to bubble and crisp, and their lust for this
was better than sex and was consummated.
I'm not, however, that strong. I close
the door on all that, I have to, forgive me,
my weakness unerringly knows
how lovely the wafer of full moon is tonight
that the sky will take eight hours
to dissolve, as if extending its pleasure
in so much golden light as long as possible;
and how my wife, who's already asleep, is somewhere
as far as Atlantis, rehearsing the songs
and performing the rituals of that otherearthly realm,
but will return to me at the appointed hour;
and how the poems in the books in my study
are part of a physics in which they hold
more space in them than they physically take up.
All this. And yet I know that there will come
a knocking at the door. A knocking, increasingly

more insistent, demanding entrance.
A knocking that won't give up.
A fist that won't retreat.
Its knuckles are bloodied but it won't retreat.

Plasterville / Occasions When Light Doesn't Function for Us

This must be how "invisibility shields"
work: you stare at something, stare at it
directly, but the light refuses
to be reflected, it skids off
(into seeming nonexistence)
on some subatomic quantum physics
banana peel—so, ocularly,
nothing's there. The future too:

its light won't travel retrograde through time.
All we can do, in our unknowing,
is confect some symbol of "maybeness"
and attempt to invest it with certainty:
the zombie apocalypse shamble-and-slaughter,
species extinction,
we-become-the-tools-of-cyborg-overlords scenario,
but also the great galactic spree of (either
disembodied or rocket-ship) travel
out to wonder-worlds like scattered pearls
against the inky deepness. . . . These
are stunt doubles standing in for what's "really"
invisibly there in tomorrow. The same

with our deaths: we *can't* see
(we don't *want* to see and so can't see)
the stopped-clock rot and oblivion
that wears our names like a pageant ribbon.
Instead (and still unbearably, but *acceptably*
unbearably) we mourn (and here
you can fill in the blank from your own increasing
obituary list) stunt doubles
taking our place in a realm where light
to see by can't escape. At Peg's memorial

I mourned for Peg, at Fran's for Fran,
at Boogie's for Boogie (the planet now
bereft of his unfailing affability),
and yet all of that time I floated *blink-blink* in and
blink-blink out of them,
these dear, sufficient substitutes.
Through them, I could pre-mourn myself.
And the past? Nobody can see the past.
"History," yes, but that's different.
Archeologists

bring us glazed ceramic bloodletting bowls
and arrowheads and crumbled baked-clay baby rattles
and theories about matrilineal inheritance—these are
canes we use
to feel out the B.C. actuality
we're blind to. In 2017, archeologists unearthed,
"from sand dunes 175 miles northwest of Los Angeles,
a five-ton sphinx of painted plaster, one of twenty
made in 1923 for the film *The Ten Commandments*."
Maybe now you too are fantasizing

a world of plaster Hebrew slaves
whip-lashed by plaster overseers as the blocks of plaster stone
are dragged across the sand to build the tomb
in which a plaster pharaoh in his coffin waits
to see if his lifelong guesses about the afterlife
hold true. Our eyes are limited to only
what the photons carry into them, and these images
have to imply the rest of the universe
that photons *don't* deliver
. . . the way that light-years, which are a measure of time,
imply light, which is timeless.

Persist

The way that Whitney Houston
could extend a final note, extend
the word inside that final note, like some
ethereal taffy being pulled out of her lungs
and up to the stars, or a wire extended
into invisibility and yet
its tensile strength would slice your heart in two . . .
that's how it is: we won't let go,
our overwhelming and formative passions
ask that we hold on to them still,
and still more, and still aftermath more,
they ache for the dig of our fingernails,
they want our tongue to fasten like a remora.
A bouquet still floats above
the long-gone shelf life date, and the contrail feathers
still embellish the sky when the jet has disappeared.
And Ishmael . . . ?
When the operatically epic voyage
ends, and the *Pequod* sinks, and all of its voices
drown, a final note still lingers,
clings like a barnacle to its rolling spar
—a persistence that carries a novel inside.

———————

Three Unalike-Like Scenarios

That lame-ass shit-on-his-dick motherfucker
goddam cheated on her *again*
with Miss Skank Waitress 2019? She will *KILL* him.
And across town, Mr. Trusting Soul just realizes
Bimbo Bitch has slipped his credit card out
of his wallet a jillionth time. . . . The thing is, though,
the scorch-your-soul thing is, that neither
of these beleaguered two can ever give up
their addictive love; and the chimera hope
of reforming the Other persists,
persists, persists, persists. . . . /

                                    In I.C.U. our friend R.
won't give up. The ward is a twenty-room-long
hush, punctuated by pompom bursts
of agonized moaning. R. won't sign
the Do Not Resuscitate form. R. won't relinquish
her love for every stained glass masterpiece
with the sun in Jesus's crown of thorns, and
picnic ant, and clawhead hammer, and book club nosh,
and mandolin string, and rivet, and divot
the planet has to offer. The tiny maze in a fresh-burst
kernel of popcorn suddenly looks as gorgeous to her
as an orchid's extravagant spirals.
She won't yield an inch;
she won't unplug the song of who she is,
or turn off the *reverb* button.
She so fiercely lusts to retain
her physical place in this physical world,
it feels counterintuitive to call it
"preparing to be a ghost."

And yet isn't that exactly what a ghost *is*?
Something that can't let go. /

And from MIT:

"Researchers have developed a system for converting all molecular
structures of proteins into audible sound that resembles musical
passages. Any protein's long sequence of amino acids becomes a
sequence of notes. Then, reversing the process, they can introduce
some variations into the music *and convert it back into proteins
never before seen in nature* [my emphasis]."

To trail a glissando across a keyboard of proteins!
Composer, year 2050: protein arpeggios!

"Different aspects of [the information by which proteins function]
can now be encoded in a form that humans are particularly well-attuned
to, [the music of] pitch, volume, and duration."

Ah. Duration.
I'm seventy-three, and if any of this
incredible bio-magic might
increase our human longevity . . .
hurry up, MIT, put a little
pep in your daily lab routine!

When R., a former
high school music teacher, finally died,
she was holding some sheet music
tightly against her chest,
and her fingers on the ruled staves
made it look as if she were playing guitar

for her last act here on the Earth.
Air guitar, I guess. And then,
in a while, she was air herself.
                            In the grave
of Queen Shub-ad at Ur, that eminence
was found on her bier with the bodies
of two women attendants positioned
"one at the head and one at the foot."
Human sacrifices. Also there,
a man's skeleton—the court harpist.
"His arm bones were still lying across
his broken instrument, with its bull's head
of gold and lapis lazuli, which
he evidently had been holding fast
even as he died."
We can't know what his music meant to him.
But we do know he wouldn't let go.

Shots

Does anybody care what it means
to the genie? Diminishing wish by wish,
gold by love by power,

until the small smoke left is anemic.
Teenage boys forever have pondered
that they're born with a limited

Fort Knox of ejaculations—isn't the word
we use for the laxity following sexual frolic
"spent"? The colonists couldn't imagine

an end to the passenger pigeon: "They cover
the Heavens by more than many Thousands, that
their clamor is of militia on the move, and the Sun

is blotted as if Night
come on us. Surely this is a wonder
almost Biblical." And yet shot by shot

that species went extinct. When it loses
a bird, the sky is that much more
exsanguinated. The sky thinks

this is how Jesus must feel
every Sunday morning, growing fainter
host by host by host.

The Point

I learned all about it in Art.
Each well-done landscape had one. It's

where every painting empties
out of itself, as through a pore-sized navel,
back into the undefinable amniotic floating
that it came from: the place

where all of the lines meet.
Yes, and in the days that followed my father's dying,
I had the idea I could find him
there, if only I could find the one
correct painting to enter: the one
where a father might wander,
having walked out from his memorial poem
in search of someplace wordless.
                                It wasn't a painting
I finally chose, but Rembrandt's etching *The Three Trees*,
I don't know why—something about the way the light
itself, the pure light of the sky, is impossibly
as shapeable as clay. For days

I traveled toward this horizon. My wife would find me
doing that, and nothing but that. She understood,
I believe, although she also worried: even in bed,
I'd have the after-storm air of the Netherlands
stirring my hair, my eyes were open only
in that world. It was for nothing: I never did
find my father. I never did reach the horizon.
I wasn't ready for that. But I did learn something
about my wife and myself, a simple surveyor's lesson
I often remember, stretched beside her in bed in the morning:
we're parallel lines. And at our individual speeds
we're heading toward the vanishing point.

Breadcrumbs Back / A Too-Curlicued Font

From the corner of my eye I see the magazine's title,
Irving
          —my father's name. For a moment the bookstore
swims around me in confounding waves. I remember
after Morgan and I divorced, when any little ding or jostle
from the world was felt as seismic, I would regularly

see her name feet-high on the sides of delivery vans
or secreted—the size of an aphid's scavengings—
in footnotes, in that click-click way the brain moves
through the overwhelming data of a day by making
constellated patterns out of our random pleasures and hurts.
Okay; but my *father?*—dead

for decades, surely any boiling need
to have the planet orbit obsessively around him
is cooled by now. And yet . . . oh, how we cherish
those stories of round-trip tickets purchased
to Oblivion City and back! The seed

discovered in a "god pot" in a pharaonic tomb:
replanted in 2017, it's sprouted
a healthy, spindly stem with healthy,
richly waxy leaves. The terrier

on the front stoop after seven years
of Who-Knows-Where. The letter sent
in January, 1877 ("an order
for spinning yarn") delivered in 2014
on the quivering current-moment tip
of 137 years of a mystery limbo. What I call

"the Hansel effect": breadcrumbs back.
It makes one imagine the elements
in the pall of greasy smoke
above the Auschwitz ovens might re-reel
back into reformed bodies, alive again
with all of their gap-tooth laughter and garlic breath
and wailing prayer and sly past-midnight winks;
or that, surreally, the whales might
swim backward until they have legs again,
and this bird the size of a kumquat might
—*hey, close your eyes for a minute, now open them up*—
BOOM, be a dinosaur, watch out! That's

crazy talk, of course. That's just poetry talk.
There isn't a nanosecond of film or a jpeg
demonstrating rust returning to iron.
Those spiky strips that keep your car, once you've entered
the rental return, from driving
in reverse?—are nothing compared
to the forces that keep us future-bound.
And my father?—I can summon poetry talk

all day, rehearsing every gooseflesh nubble
on his stretched neck as he shaved
in the bathroom mirror, young and resilient
and full of what seemed like a magic vitality
he worked up every morning before going off
to another ten-hour day of hustle and diminution,
but the single ritual shovelful of dirt
I dropped onto his casket lid
is the heaviest thing in the universe,
the weight of a black hole is silly in comparison,
and the truth is even Lazarus

couldn't have beat with any success against
that horizontal door. Nor is Morgan

going to appear on my stoop from Who-Knows-Where;
or my sister's breasts regenerate, here
on the other side of the surgeon's dutiful knife.
Although if you want to read

about how the starfish manages it, there's an article
in this *Scientific American* up on the shelf
right next to . . . oh.
                                   Oh.
Living.

I suppose he is, yes I suppose he is,
if my memory counts.

Astronomy Song, with Confusions

An earlier version of this obituary misstated the name of Mr. Hoagland's
first poetry collection. It is "Sweet Ruin," not "Sweet Rain."

—*The New York Times*

They look, they *are*, so unapproachable
and indifferent; still, it's because of the stars
that sometimes we don't even know if we're suffering

or easing over the borderline into a day
of lazy contentment. We're created
from their energy and matter, as you know, and so
what we would see as major realignments
of those ur-components (Democrat/ Republican
for example, Bird of Paradise / piranha
for example) they would understand
as equivalent Big Bang units
indistinguishably shaped. And you can tell me
that the woman who's wrestled her camel

finally, strenuously, onto the sand and sheltered
against the coming simoom in the part-enclosing nook
of its belly, the camelstink rising as heavy now
as prongs inside her nostrils . . . and the woman being paid
a thousand dollars tonight for Super Rap Dude X
to snort a line of champagne-quality cocaine
from the velvety valley between her breasts

. . . are many galaxies apart in degree,
in basic Homo sapiens degree, but go ahead, tell that
to the stars comprising Andromeda, see if their spectra
blink by a single potassium molecule,
shout it, go ahead. The ink
of King's "I have a dream" oration / the ink

of *Mein Kampf*. Use astral
measurements, and sex and death are closer

than the breathing pores along the sides of a cockroach
and the "great red spot" on Jupiter, which are brother and sister
atoms, after all. By astral metrics,
sex and death are twined irrevocably and the same

electrochemical substrata hold
them both. And yet we know, we *know*,
the difference. Our lowest depravity
(remember that night? remember that thought
that night?) and our saintliest innocence . . .
we *know*—duh—how to tell one from the other; but don't
expect Betelgeuse to care. The genome,

the same genome, was lizard
then bird then gill-thing in the womb and now
is you; and *I'm* amazed, but don't look to Cassiopeia
to grovel at that or do jumping jacks.
Public and private?—every one of us,
whether painfully or with suavity, bilocates
here-there-here a hundred times across a day, although
we're homogenous substances to the Milky Way.
Oh really? You can have this arm

I'm writing with, stars, if you'll keep my wife
—my singular, unduplicatable wife—
from harm. My wife in the light,
my wife in the indigo thunderstorm.

It's a monstrous thought, I know:

to the laws of thermodynamics, evil and good
are identical twins.

Depending on the metric, error
might not exist: mistakes imply comparatives at work,
but the stars are inclined to see
all forms as Form; if we want to be people
and not some pure embodiment of "astral stuff,"
we might have to cherish mistakeness.
It could be that we're never dead any more

than we're alive; it's all just cyclic recombinings
of at Oort cloud's (Google it) elements
with some one-way-or-another physics
giving a directional tilt to the mix. That may
be true, but it has little to do

with mourning or with pleasure—really *anything*
we call "human" and feel owns us
overwhelmingly in the groin, or the meaty cathedral
we label "the heart," or our pinprick tear ducts.
Today I was thinking of Tony Hoagland

and the rain came down,
no the sun, no the rain, oh the sweet,
the ruinous, the sweet, sweet rain.

A Tough Day Begins with a Stupid Joke

Gianna fell and so much broke
we joke she should open
a brokerage firm. Haha, although
I'm seriously tired

of the pain up close in *my* life
through my friends' lives:

R, who married M
at that bar on Douglas wearing a kilt
and I don't know what he wore or didn't
under that, but I know it's where
the cancer began to flower
and the chemo—like any other
chemical pesticide—began its war
against that monstrous blossoming,
in the trenches of battleground R. And also

S with her recent Alzheimer's,
like a long chord in the concert hall
as it starts to lose coherence.
I could go on. But really

you could go on, you don't need *me*
to compile a list of these doors
in the hallways of pain, with the names
of people we know in gilt lettering.
Their suffering distracts
from all of the other remorseless varieties

we can imagine. The pain of looking
—probably wistfully at first, but then more like
a heated iron rod in your heart—

at the Ark as it slides away
on the rising water and the rains begin
to pellet down even harder. The pain

of light in the infinity of empty space
when there's nothing
to land on, to touch, when there's nothing
—a planet, a mote of dust—by which
to prove you exist: *that's*
loneliness. But these examples

are frivolous, when there's ambulance-wail
somewhere every minute. The point is,
I'm sick of how it hides out
in "piano," with that "o" in there
as if an ode
to hospice care
or those surgery tents near the enemy lines
got dropped and rearranged.

I'm sick of how it's always waiting
in a neuron in the brain, is waiting
expectantly to be called forth, the way
the shattering waits inside
the delicate glass of a goblet
for the high note of release. I'm tired of listening

to its murmurous almost-voice
that follows us everywhere, in the shadows,
around a corner, and tired of how our deepest
agonies are only its caprice. Last night
I passed a house a few blocks over, and
out of a curtained second-floor window issued

an ongoing series of screeches—a child, I think—
that seemed to bypass my ears and go
straight to my spinal fluid. The helplessness
and dread that exist below language.

Let's forget all that for a while. Perhaps
a bottle of five-star wine
and a flakily fresh baguette
at the bistro, outside on its terrace,
in the light the shade trees sift for us
until only a golden benediction is left.
And even here. Is it me? Is it only *me*?
I'm tired of how
French calls bread "pain."

Tough Day: Closure

Upstairs, in the bath, my wife
is humming some made-up tune
in which the mood of a zoned-out
happiness willfully prevails.

Why do I suddenly think of the horse skull
that I saw last year in the countryside?

Because a bird rose out of it,

as if the brain
is determined to sing and fly,
the brain is determined to sing and fly
no matter what.

Touching on Recent American History*

(Spring–Summer–Fall 2020, and other moments)

*the title comes from a 1970 anthology
of poems edited by Robert Bly

My American Times

We say "chevron," we say "arrowing"
and "vee," we set them crossing "sky-blue silk," and then

the geese land; and as if demoted from that
imperial beauty, they waddle like comic

middle-class shoppers at a salad bar
(All You Can Eat!), their feather duster rumps

awaggle, here at Riverside Park. Whatever
oracular power their honking seemed to have had

in flight becomes the playground blat of tricycle horns.
In either of those modes, though, what astonishes me

today—another dismal day in July of 2020—
is how oblivious they are to the great momentum

of my human times, my American times, and the place
of my friends within those vectors: Livia reports

that Bimbim's COVID-19 led to a tracheotomy
"and three weeks later he's still in ICU

on a ventilator," burbling, fighting; Jimbo's
kids were rubber bulleted at a protest march

"and the wounds look just like radiation lesions";
and the economy; and the sequestering; and the loss

of public civility; of privacy; and our exodus
into the land of constant belittling; and the sense

some might have had in Pompeii as the first smutch
blotted the sun, or some might have had at the harbor

witnessing the casks of British tea heaved overboard
with riotous whoops . . . the sense that some

realigning was beginning, and their world would change.
But the geese ignore all that; it isn't in them

to communicate with us, to extend or withhold some small
forgiveness, to commiserate: their hearts are AA batteries

dead to our wavelength. They have less
to do with us than I have language for. Less even

than ghosts—which, after all,
are the spectrally eggy extensions of the glories and shames

of our lordly, our compromised,
maddening, seething, pleasureful and excruciated

flesh; and of the glories and shames
of our psyches. Less than even the stars:

our every constituent element was born inside
their thermonuclear cores. But the geese exist

in another dimension
altogether. Some of us witnessed the triumphant

touch of the first *Homo sapiens* foot-down on the moon;
and some of clustered on the beach in 1513,

staring perplexedly as the horse-men singularities
(demons? gods?) approached through the surf

to the susceptible, sandy edge of the Aztec empire.
To the geese it's all

non-goose, just that; if even that. However
the night of the day on which I wrote the foregoing

I had (it might have been the "loss of privacy"
thought that did it) this dream: in the dream I awoke

to a minimal but insistent humming
that registered less as a sound in the ear

and more as a shirr in the blood.
There was a drone outside my window, a metallic black

that blended, like intentional camo, into the night.
A spy drone. About the size of a bird. It hovered there

at the height of the sill on the second floor
and then /a flash/ it crashed to the ground

and lay there, bent. I warily walked outside.
A thin smoke rose from its seams, and the kind of scent when the air

is alive with voltage. A small dome opened.
In it, nested by Frankensteinian tangles of wires,

its power source was revealed: the brain of a goose.
A living walnut shape with a feeble pulse.

"You see?" I heard it say faintly.
"You see? I do care.

Just not in the way that you wanted."

————————

The Taino did not have writing but they did have government. "They have their laws gathered in ancient songs, by which they govern themselves," Pané reported. They sang their laws, and they sang their history.

—Jill Lepore

Autumn: from some weather channel
a thousand miles inside of themselves,

the geese receive the broadcast, and answer
the call. And in a day

they're gone. They rise as a single
sinuous ribbon of goose from the river, then shape themselves

without thought for their aerodynamic, long,
long journey south. And in the vacancy

they leave behind, I think of that Jill Lepore quotation,
and think of them: is it possible

to hear their strident signaling,
their unmistakable back-and-forth communiqués,

as talk in which the laws of their kind
—their justice, and its promises and its limitations—

are argued and signed off on? Bird song
in general: the robin now, and now the jay:

what manifestos and codicils and amendments fill
what we perceive as lyric outpourings

of avian delight? On a day when the news feed
in my America is cars on fire;

buildings on fire; a three-year-old with a drive-by bullet
lodged in her chest as if tagging her crumpled-up body

for delivery to God; and also a cop dead; and a protestor
dead; and almost nobody weeping for them, instead

nitpicking the video for which one threw
a fist first; and a nurse in a hospital virus annex

kneeling in the hallway there, unable to rise
and face (in her mask) another day of too

too too too much . . . we could do worse, I think, than governance
by music. And we have. Oh, I know: this is only

poetry jabber. Empty froufrou words. The terms of jurisprudence
as sung by the oriole, the edicts of the wren,

lala, lafuckingla. Who cares? But, still . . .
what politician would I ever trust, who isn't moved by their

congressional lala discourse? And the whales' songs,
that travel miles—maybe many dozens of miles—

across the sea, that can shiver the fringes of continents
. . . these songs might be their version of the ponderous

slabs of stone on which the Law Code of Hammurabi
was inscribed: a great, fraught legislative weight

that floats on the waters the way that feathers and leaves do
—effortlessly.

Actual Stature

Holly, who works in "aerospace flowmatics testing,"
says after hours she'll set the wind tunnel

"to 'bearable'" and jog in there: it's good
to have her ramped-up heartbeat lost

inside a greater sound, "it keeps things
in proportion, it reminds me." Though she doesn't say

of *what*, we know implicitly it's of
our actual stature

in the universe. It's useful to remember what
the guy out today in Riverside Park

with his metal detector understands: he shows me,
still begrimed from six inches under, a dime

from 1810 and two malt-color musket balls
that are flattened ("they connected

with *something*, alright") at either end.
"If you think *these*

is amazing—*Kansas
used to be a friggin' ocean!*" . . . the awareness Holly

brings us: that we walk above the skeletons of creatures
the size of an amphitheater

where *Hamlet* could be performed and an intimate audience
have enough room to camp on the floor;

our heart's toy knocks would be inaudible
against the massive boom of that immensosaur's. Or look up,

and it's the same: the stars. Or turn to art: that fisherman
in the rowboat, in the corner, is so tiny

against the monolithic wall of mist and hint
of background mountains—he could even be mistaken

for an error the painter has yet to let
blend back invisibly

into the air. Today, a day of protest hellfires
set in the streets of my country's cities, I'm

so small, and my friends so small
—inconsequential—against

that violent overwhelm.
People are dying. People

on both emphatic sides of this
are dying—even as the spraypaint messages tell us

each life is invaluable. I hold my wife
in my arms; lub-dub, lub-dub. Right now

on the video feed, a cop car rushes off.
Its flasher, nightmare-red and rhythmic,

like some cardiovascular warning
on a hospital monitor, owns our rapt attention

for a moment; and then dwindles of course
with distance; and then disappears totally into the night.

Invisible: A Partial Survey

The three-year-old thinks if she closes her eyes
she's invisible to everyone.
In Shakespeare's day, the peachfuzz boy (the actor)
was invisible-cum-visible
inside the woman (the role). Or was it the woman
(the role) was invisible-cum-visible inside
the boy (the actor)? In Hitler's day
my grandparents—dirty Jews—
attempted to will themselves invisible
for simply walking down a public street, and chose
their nondescript attire with the care of those who know
the merest slip-up could be fatal: her babushka
was determindedly as drab as spit.
The diary of Philip Henslowe (proprietor
of the Rose and Fortune theaters in Shakespeare's day),
amid a list of props and wardrobes, mentions
"a robe for to go invisible." (Lost
technology? How many billions of tax dollars
would the Pentagon hand over for just one hour alone
with that robe!) Although why *any* piece of clothing
was required for such transformation
is mystifying: *The Oxford Shakespeare*
says, discussing Elizabethan theater conventions,
"Oberon and Prospero have only to declare themselves
invisible to become so." Playing, *zaydee*
scrunches his eyes shut: "Mishaleh, where
did you *go*? Don't hide from me!": and the three-year-old
is rapturously transported into giggles,
every time. I think the zeitgeist is invisible
to almost everybody, when they're *in* it: it's only
in retrospect that Einstein's light
and Joyce's Ulyssean fractal language and Curie's
capable hands (and glowing fingertips [and her cookbook's

glowing pages!]) herald
the undoing of a universe, so a new one,
indeterminate and quantum, can be born; but with
the three-year-old running a fever, and the bank
up your ass about payments: that transforming überspirit is lost
from sight, its wavelengths too incomprehensible to fit
one's daily gaze. That silly little man
with the laughable moustache, swaggering and bellicose . . .
it turns out, German three-year-olds ran fevers
too, and the everyday business of German banks was just
as everyday pitiless; as with most of us, that's
attention-absorbing enough: we don't need to answer the knock
of politics at the door. A moth is camouflaged
in *month*; perversely, real fun is invisible
in *funeral*; I am a weakish speller,
William Shakespeare. The play that he and John Fletcher
authored together, *The History of Cardenio?* . . . not one word
has come down to us, only the title shimmers enticingly
at the edge of our visible spectrum. The eponymous
invisible man in H. G. Wells's seminal novel can bandage his body
head-to-toe to be noticeable, and it's fair to say
that mummy wrappings did the same for Egyptian souls,
the *ka*, the *ba*, that otherwise would be no more in evidence
than ours. It's fair to say that Wells's novel is invisible
but there, inside—or hovering over—Ralph Ellison's
Invisible Man, another seminal novel and a reminder that
the zeitgeist of our early-to-middle twentieth century
—Gertrude Stein, Picasso, John Cage,
the stork-steps-and-spirals radicalism of Martha Graham—meant
dogpoop to an African-American porter,
washer woman, reefer hustler . . . all, the color
(or non-color, really) of nothingness, to the dominant culture.
Sue Storm of The Fantastic Four can turn herself see-through

—a nifty superhero capability—as could
her newspaper comics predecessor, Invisible Scarlet O'Neil
(1949-1954), whose power was gained
from poking a finger into a ray of light
in her scientist-father's lab. (And Wonder Woman's airplane,
you'll remember, is transparent.) In Nazi Germany,
invisible spies were present in so many households:
the children—the *children!*—redone by the state
into skulking, hidden betrayers of their own family.
Sinclair Lewis's novel about a demagogue taking control
of America is titled *It Can't Happen Here*. Oh, but it can,
it can when our backs are turned, and our eyes are focused close up
on the harvest, the marriage, the drug, the God, the doctor's report,
the earworm jingle. "Djinn," "ghosts," "spirits": every culture
has some. (Maybe some are around you now.) Abstractions
are visible only when implemented. Vacuum. Neutrinos.
Life in another galaxy. "Secret writing" in lemon juice
(but the heat of a match will reveal it). The actual source
of the funding behind the anonymous donations behind
the series of smear campaign ads. And let's not forget
Mr. Superinvisible, 1970 piece of cinema schlock. One morning
zaydee's eyes are scrunched shut, *zaydee*
still and pale, *zaydee* in the long dark box,
and his eyes won't open no matter how long she cries,
no matter if everybody cries; and some presentiment, some gray wing
of a thirty-year-old's knowledge of the human condition,
momentarily brushes the mind of the three-year-old.
I'm seventy-three: and, trust me, most days I'm completely invisible
to the twenty-year-old waitresses of the world;
and my wife—my lovely, vital sixty-six-year-old wife—endures
her versions of the same [insert emoji here
of a dead white male waving for attention]. And perhaps
to the mineral eyes of a mountain, the ozone eyes

of seraphs, we're as not-here (all of us,
all of the time) as the space of a hummingbird's flapping wings
we can't believe is real. Of Shakespeare,
Bill Bryson says, "Except that he was certainly productive,
nothing of note can be stated with certainty
about [his] life from 1603 to 1607" . . . four full years, as gone
as the magician's assistant is gone when the crimson coverlet
gets whisked away. And Dorothy Soer
and Ann Lee: they were named
along with Shakespeare in a court injunction in 1596,
but "who the women were is quite unknown . . . they
have never been identified or even plausibly guessed at."
In 1593 the British government spent £12,000—a fortune—
in order to spy on its own citizens.
And the Jews of Nazi Germany? . . . whisked away,
along with Gypsies and homosexuals. Some used to live
on this very block, some used to deliver their goods
in a slightly slant-bodied wagon
their children would shyly peek from: big,
black currant eyes in sweetly doughy faces.
Now they're ashes. It's fair to say sometimes
I see that country folded invisibly into my America.
Or is it unfair to posit that? I know good people
were waiting in line in Germany at the baker's,
and were pinning up their wash to dry,
and inflating a bicycle tire, and opening
the morning paper to skim its news—people
as good as you, as me.
They didn't see it coming.

Secret Life

This mailbox on a Washington, D.C. corner is—no,
not in this story it isn't. Here, it's the unsuspicious
surface on which Aldrich Ames—chief of the CIA's
Soviet counterintelligence branch—would chalk the signals
he used for meeting up with his KGB handlers. Nine years,
Ames worked as a mole for Moscow, and the damage
he created included a number of executions. I've
arranged this so that we're following him on an appropriate
Indian summer day—a false man in false weather.
He's on his way to the mailbox, passing the house
where Stanley [redacted] lives, assistant day custodian
at Consolidated Hogworks, although also (in his secret life)
the rich, chick-magnet King of the online nation Stanistan;
and passing the house of Miss W., the neighborhood
Meals-on-Wheels lady, who moonlights in her latex
as Mistress Salacia—money! orgasm! power! And
this poem is about their—no, this poem, this bees adrift
in the false-news summer clover, is a masquerade too.
It's really about when he passes my door.
It's really about when he passes you.

Toward a Crest

In the reign of Charles I, a book required a royal "licenture" in order to be published. John Aubrey reports that Thomas Hobbes presented Charles with his *History of England from 1640 to 1660*, "which the King has read and likes extreamly, but tells him there is so much truth in it he dares not license for feare of displeasing the Bishops."

Ah—yes. Too much truth. My friend D is *finally*-finally
finalizing his year-long-fussed-at manuscript of poems
before submission. In a single line out of over one hundred pages,
he notes that a fourteen-year-old boy's late-night awareness
of the fourteen-year-old girls just a cabin away from his
at summer camp is "sexual." Three female friends
have suggested he change the word, "*They* don't have a problem
with it [*they* aren't mired parochially in limitation,
not them], but each one knows *another* woman who would
[etc., etc.], and so I'm thinking of substituting" . . . what?
(and why am *I* dragged in as a troubleshooting reviser?)
"hormonal," "fecundity-heavy"? (*Ugh.*) And truth

is much on my mind (and, truthfully, yours too)
now, in our lint-speck of historical time. Behind D,
on a screen of real-time news, a woman's professional mouth
(that's pixels of a mouth) is recapping the spill a man's
professional political mouth let out of itself a few
lint-minutes earlier. Already its words are decomposing
into their constituent prevarication-units (the war lie,
the graft lie, the economy lie, a list as disturbingly long as his earlier
list of campaign promises) and, if Pinocchio's wood nose works
the way a Geiger counter does—but substituting
the breaking down of truth for the degrading of uranium—
its famous telltale lengthening could be kept active

in DC twenty-four seven. As if it isn't enough
the "blue sky" isn't blue, it's just the way that we

perceive the "wavelength scattering" up above in what we call
"the sky" (and what, for that matter, we call "up"). And
the cardinal isn't red, it isn't *intrinsically* red:
the "red" is the light it refuses. The stars *don't* twinkle; that's
a myth told by the atmosphere. We think we're solid, but mainly
we're as empty as the emptiness the wind plays ghostly
music with, in the alders. Then there's scam-bait
after scam-bait in your laptop, on your phone,
phish phish, a salted gold mine waiting every time
you tap a key. "It isn't only," I say to D,

"a matter of sound and rhythm, it's that 'sexual'
is more *honest*": that for fourteen-year-old boys (*and* girls)
the tidal wave and magnesium flare, the whole
full-on enormity-confusion-and-compulsion of sex
and its grandeur and harshness and holiness and mysteries,
is shovel-whacks to the head each seven seconds, and
a jillion years of fine-tuned evolution *wants it so*.
"There's nothing wrong in acknowledging that." Well,
sure, D says with a look (but not in words).
Well, sure, but you know, says the look: "*for feare
of displeasing the Bishops.*" On my way home, I think
of the feather—the Feather of Truth, of *ma'at*—

the animal-headed gods of ancient Egypt kept in the farther pan
of the balance at the gateway to the Afterlife, and
the dead man's heart—with its life-accumulation
of deceptions—was set in the other pan, was weighed
in final judgment, and he was either found acceptable
for Eternity or was, on the spot, obliterated by something
called the Devourer, which evidently has a taste for souls.
A game: Would person X's soul be deemed immortal
or be dog chow? Say, the President's. Congressman A's or Z's.
Grifters, hoaxers, shysters. In the old days they

would rent an entire fake stock broker's office
—furnished! a dozen employees!—for a juicy con. Today

they have all of infinity—the internet *is* infinite, yes?—
and the Oval Office. How would my mother fare
in that game of scrutinizing balance pans? I don't think
there was ever a human being more decent
than Fannie Goldbarth—once she sent me back
to a five-and-dime because the cashier accidentally
handed me ten cents too much in change—and if
her fuss-budget life of lower-lower-middle-class worries
didn't allow for scrupulousness displayed on a level
of Vegas playas or dotcom entrepeneurs,
her moral worth, if small, was solid: she could beat
a cheating butcher to pulp with that brick. And yet

she must have lied a dozen times a day the way
we all, in our human confoundedness, do
(the doctor says you'll feel "some discomfort" [meaning
"pain"]; the Red Marauder and Marco the Cannibal
trade body flops and neck locks in a "real" match
we know—we're all complicit—is as scripted
as a pas de deux at the National Ballet). Me too:
my friend's initial *isn't* D. Welcome to where I live,
on Flimflam Lane, in Swindle City. (I could go on:
the state bird is a mocking bird, etc.) One part
of our mind lies to the rest of the mind and the body, but
despite its silky eloquence, we *aren't* immortal. It

is, however, a beautiful delusion. And we're born
with such "fecundity-heavy" instincts!—how
could it all give out? When I visit my parents' graves,
their lower-lower-middle-class stone nubbins

that ask for remembrance . . . what I see are the graves
they deserve—monumental, marble—these two people who
(whether the Mayor of Chicago or their teenage son)
were infallible bullshit detectors. (They
could body-cavity-search a person's conscience: politicians,
look out!) If life were just, and accurate,
these graves would exhibit a family crest: an X,
made of a wooden nose and an ancient Egyptian feather.

Sad Song, Two Girls

When the thoughts come . . . there are pills
for that, "away machines," some white, some red,

or there used to be. The homegirl who provided them
got three years, and her man got dead.

And what will she do without them now
—what will whisk her away instead?

Now one is in jail—actual bars.
And one is in jail—her actual head.

Undercover Cop

He spent a year in the gang, he shared their every violent
pleasure. Once he watched as they drove nails into the palms
of two factory watchmen.

                     That year's over. Ah; but *is* it?

There are people who can lick a sick thrill, light it, stroke it,
casually—then turn away, unmuddied, to their civil selves.
There's a novel's-worth of detail in that idea, but this
asks no more than to be a lyric poem, to be a moment
one year later, when his sassy six-year-old won't shut
the fuck up, and he finds his arm—his gentle, father arm—
upraised and ready for the hard arc down. His own arm . . .
something's *really* there, that seems to have entered his system
as surely as if it were caught from a needle.

Lincoln

Arnie's father, fifty-six, called at 6 a.m. "in pain,
and he *never* admits to pain": the daycare nurse
fucked up the catheter cleanse, and his kidneys
ballooned with urine overnight. That afternoon,
3:30, Arnie was booked for a lawyer consultation:
his wife, who he loved, and whom he *still* loved,
was divorcing him, from *her* bed
in the oncology wing of the hospital where his father
was being recatheterized. These days

when we say "tipping point," we mean the phrase
as climate change, pollution, species death, perhaps
the economy, but there's a tottery, ever-jostling
atom-diameter fulcrum up in everybody's head, where
over-scale loads are duly weighed: I think of it
as atom-Arnie deep in every Arnie, and
as atom-you-and-me in you and me,
and when it shifts and slips,
the greater life around it shifts and slips.
Let's simply say he didn't need,
and handle easily, the car's flat tire
at 3:00 that grayly raining afternoon. And Arnie's

specialty at the local U is American History, notably
the Civil War. He once said, "I can lecture
about the 750,000 Americans who died: the very
enormity is a counterweight to emotion.
But show me the photograph of a single
seven-year-old daughter clambering a mound of corpses
in search of her father, lifting a detached arm
like a damp baton, to double-check if the ring on it
is her father's. . . ." Twice, he wept at that
in the lecture hall and had to be led away.
And so I drove out in the rain,

and helped in my own dumb all-thumbs way
with the tire, and took him, not to his lawyer's,
but to the clinic where his therapist works.
"Meltdown," I said by way of explanation
to the receptionist. "I prefer," said Arnie,
"'a little disequilibrium.'" He's better
now. And he showed me his meds to prove it.
He lined them up on the desk in two rows
facing each other, as if for a battle.
The Bring-Him-Higher pills
and the Bring-Him-Back-Down-Again pills.
The blue and the gray.

———————

When Nella wakes from her chemotherapy

fog, and the whirling world around her decides
what its center is,
it's Nella. 24-7 Nella. Which is,
of course, as it *should* be, under the circumstances,
harsh as they are. There may be satellites of hers
in orbit—satellite Arnie, satellite
all of the goobers back at the office—okay, but
let *them* open a vein for the doctors
to pour in a burning dose of their purge.
When she's calm again, and clear, there's a small
I-think-I-can-keep-it-down dinner, there's a message
from her lawyer, there's a sense in fact
that life goes on, the pandemic goes on,
the protests—this is the summer of 2020—continue,
peaceful sometimes, sometimes however with heads
broke open and spilling their jello onto the street.
Heads—and hearts.
America goes on. Out the window

the nighttime streets are darkness
having its skull punched by the small quick fists
of flashers and sirens;
ambulances, she thinks—this *is* a hospital—but,
she knows from the news feeds scrolling over
her laptop and the room's overpowering t.v. screen,
police cars too, maybe National Guard
or even, she's heard, the Army. As if anyone
can take for fact what's heard, these days
of clamor and artful conniving. Soon,
some farther, formerly darker part
of the night is lit with the ghastly flicker
of what the news loop tells her is a fire

born of decency and looting, like two sticks
some manic Boy Scout's rubbed together.
She doesn't sob at the numbers
the well-groomed newsroom wonk spouts out
—her empathy center is pretty numb right now—
but when the image is of a single child
crawling out of a tumble of burning boards, she
sobs, alright; and thinks of Arnie

and thinks of the Civil War, and the knotted-up complexities
surrounding it, that Arnie so often (interestingly
sometimes; sometimes decidedly not) would yak about,
"The conflict was to free the slaves," "The conflict
mainly was economic," "The role Great Britain played,"
"The Congressional clashes over states' rights,"
"The distribution of Kevlar vests to militia," oh
wait, that last one is from five minutes ago,
she's foggy again, red fire in the sky
is in her mind the way a speck of blood was
centered in the egg yolk that her mother served her
thirty years ago . . . she slides to sleep

as if by now the sirens function
as a lullabye. The sirens. . . .
The shrill of bugles alerting the cavalry. . . .
We're all living through "American history."
We just happen to call it "now."

———————

750,000 dead.
(And that's ignoring of course the plantation slaves,
who were dying prodigiously anyway.)
I don't know if Lincoln would have had the exact count

when he boarded the train for Gettysburg
to deliver, in his reedy voice,
270 words of dedication,
but the ledger in his marrow implicitly knew,
and it released that number
unceasingly into his orbiting blood.
An unthinkable number
—at least, back then.
Quoting Jill Lepore in her book *These Truths*:

"Ulysses S. Grant said a man could walk
across the battlefield in any direction
without touching the ground but only the dead.
They died in heaps, they were buried in pits."
Yet after his eighty-mile train ride,
arriving at the station nearest to Gettysburg,
where soldiers' coffins were still untidily piled,
the number

that threatened to unsteady him, to tilt him over
into a disequilibrium, was:
one. He delivered his brief and eloquent
burial ground oration
"still in mourning for his own young son."
*. . . we here highly resolve that these dead
shall not have died in vain. . . .*

More numbers:
Lincoln was fifty-six
when John Wilkes Booth assassinated him
at 10:15 p.m.
on April 14 (Good Friday),
six blocks from the White House.
The funeral train with his casket
weaved across the country
for twelve days and nights.
And when it finally stopped
on May 4, 1865,
the pallbearers carried the casket
one thousand miles,
one thousand somber miles

into the brain of Mary Todd Lincoln,
and rested it on one atom in there.

July 2020

Manly interned with a crusading publisher in a small town in Kansas.
The publisher had taken on the Klan. So it was Manly and this publisher,
working together against the Klan, which was quite powerful at the time.
The first thing that the publisher offered him, after Manly had taken the
job, was Manly's choice of an automatic pistol or a revolver.

—from a reminiscence of writer Manly Wade Wellman,
shortly after World War I, by David Drake

This month my cell phone's inbox for texts
is Misery Central Headquarters. Don is waiting
the results of his CT scan, to find out about the lumps
transgressing across his liver.
Chris: the bone marrow test. Then Carly: should she sue,
since the hospital staff admitted that Tina's oncologist
overdosed her on chemo, which is why her blood began
to disappear and what remained in her system
clotted. And Barbo's mother fell, "fell bad,"
and, well, at *her* age. . . . In a time when the news

is incessantly pandemic and protests,
pandemic and protests, pandemic and protests,
following us all day and into our sleep like the recording
of a drum corps set on infinity loop,
I'm suddenly reminded that the classic griefs,
the millennia-old and overly familiar
reasons to sob and rage, still show up
at the door and face our heated jeremiads
with a cool sneer. There are more, too—cruel betrayals
from our bodies by the handful—but I'll spare you

and simply ask the question: *How to face such overmuch
bad news?* and then offer the only answer I know:

One night, after midnight, when Manly had finished putting
that day's paper to bed, and was about to descend
the narrow alley stairs from the second (editorial offices) floor,
he heard some furtive movements—more than one man lurking,
clearly—in the alley below, and a voice said, "Come on down,
kid. We've got something important to talk to you about."
Manly fed a round into his .32. "No, *you* come *up*.
Who's first?" But no one volunteered; and soon they slunk off.

Take them one at a time, Albert; one at a time.

Amazing Stories

When *Amazing Stories*, the first all-science-fiction magazine, ceased publication, its torch was taken up by *Astounding, Astonishing, Startling, Fantastic, Marvel, Thrilling Wonder, Galaxy, Cosmos, Other Worlds*.

—a history of science fiction

To the American cosmologist and UFO sceptic Carl Sagan, the way that most of the aliens people claim to encounter today strongly resemble humans in their basic morphology is simply down to "a failure of the imagination" and "a preoccupation with human concerns" upon behalf of abductees. As he put it: "Not a single being presented in these accounts is as astonishing as a cockatoo would be if you had never before beheld a bird."

—S. D. Tucker

Nothing Stranger Happens on the Dark Side of the Moon

than on the dark side of the eyelids.

Science Fiction

As the 1920s progressed . . . many amateur radio hams, particularly young boys still naive enough to not know any better, [had] the idea that they might . . . make first contact with Mars whilst fiddling about with the dials.

—S. D. Tucker

And so it turns out there were two beliefs,
both wrong. That their messages might reach Mars.
That there were Martians to listen. And
for most of us, one incorrect assumption is more
than enough. That she still loves him
after all these years. That he doesn't have a second, secret
bank account. And still, their fourteen-year-old son in the attic
is happy, working his glowing dials like a high priest.
(Okay, a *third* belief: it helps that the attic
is "closer to Mars.") Both parents love this boy,
and so it sort of works: they all travel together
obligingly into the future,
with a faith that they'll find signs of life
and share some common language.

It wasn't only fourteen-year-olds.
Some of "the best minds of today!" suggested
a thousand miles of twenty-five-feet-high mirrors
through the Sahara, or great lit trenches shaped like pi,
to make contact. "How will we ever know
if we don't *try?*" (Cue in the Wright brothers,
Galileo, Sojourner Truth.) And in some isotope
of *this* poem, in some parallel cosmos, the parents
do try—marriage counseling, weekend getaways,
prayer; whatever. Maybe there, the headlines announce

world peace, and imminent sources of free, clean energy
for everyone. That isn't *this* poem,
of course; but it's not an impossible poem
—so long as the parallel cosmos exists.

———————

Turns out, there are no princesses on Mars
or green-skinned warriors. Turns out, Martian scientists aren't
electrifying the skies with atomic-frizzling gizmos.
Disappointing. And everybody is born to die, no matter
how much you love them. *Very* disappointing.
The sun too: will die. We could "turns out" ourselves
repeatedly until we sat here numb to any
lilt or prickle, but what's the point of that?
Try this belief: the poor are the Good Lord's way
of allowing charity. This: in order for Paradise
to arrive, a devastating war or pestilence first needs to undo us.
Turns out, there are sillier things than being fourteen
in an attic, with a radio, with the belief that there's a wavelength
that will open you up to the universe.

Exist

A net, a colander . . . the nothing
is the part that makes it work.
And thus the marriage of (everyone

loved to say it) Phil in Philly and Sandy
in San Diego: it was crossing
the Great Plains emptiness that made
their weekends glorious.
And thus the unthinkable void of outer space

we require so gods can live
in a realm befitting their stature,
and can juggle all of those classic unknowns
—Death, and Where We Come From, etc.—
without awkwardly elbowing lesser matters;
and so the arbitrary patterns we fashion up there
—a Dipper, a Hare—to keep us from going
crazy under unboundaried vacuum: the patterns
require the vacuum.
We've looked out to the stars;

and down to the increasingly infinitesimal zeroes
inside what's inside
of the atom; and we've watched (we've enabled)
ourselves become the new non-substance
pixel-us;
and the news brought back is worrisome:

we're barely here, we're barely "we,"
the wind hits more as it crosses the Arctic wastes
than it does in the nullity of our bodies.
"You're Nothing," the mountain-top Zen mystic says,

"give in to the Nothing, *be* the Nothing," as if
that's the ultimate goal. And yet
when I stare in Sarah's eloquent eyes
in Sarah's mute (because of the breathing tube) face
in ICU, I can see that here,
on the brink, Nothing is the last thing
that she wants to be. Because of this,

when Phil and Sandy leave her room
and its beeping apparatus, they go home
to a weekend of stroking each other's skin
as if solidity is actual, and dependable, and joy
has weight and texture.

Ex nihilo, "out of nothing."
The way some people see the Virgin Mary
in quartz or bark or pancakes;
and at one time people saw canals
striated across the surface of Mars, irrigating

the fields where surely workers tended
the Martian wheat, where pipes relayed
the drinking water to Martian homes
and arenas and palaces and temples where
the Martian high priests gathered, finding gods
in shards of Martian granite and Martian schist,
and observatories where scientists studied
Earth and argued if we exist.

Inside

A jay lands on the ceramic planter
—delft-blue perched on umber—
and regards me, in what *I* see
as a series of separate nanosecond head-jerks,
though the problem is I see too slow
to follow what, for the jay, is a casual smoothness.
Add it to Goldbarth's List of Endless Wonders
and Mysteries. Along with the bird we dissected
in high school bio lab: that small corpse fit in my hand
but its dizzying inside extended for miles.
Along with dreams my wife has every night
just inches away from me
—as indecipherable and opaque
as the stone thoughts in the Sphinx's head.

———————

Today the results of Chris's
bone marrow biopsy are due by noon.
Yesterday, Jimbo's dad received
a twelfth stent—they rose into the heart
through a micro-slit in his groin.
My only touchstone for these is the surgery
on my prostate: snipping, rearranging
what remains with a wild,
guesswork abandon. My only touchstone
for *that* is the car repair shop
up the block: four guys bent
to an opened-up engine, scratching
their heads in perplexity at its secret temples
and alien gods.

———————

When Annie emerged from the anesthesia
she said, "Too bad I don't remember
what it was like on that planet I visited."

When I think of us as the final sum
of ten thousand unknowns,
I see we're like the moon
—if it carried its dark side
inside.

How will we get to Mars
and live in lovely domed and spired cities there,
when we know so little
about what's close
—what sleeps beside us
and in us.

Survey: Better Mousetrap

One might have thought that merely being five was ample
reason . . . but no, as Dr. Immanuel Kipnis attempted
valiantly to inveigle out of my ear the lost dry pea
that I'd insinuated so irretrievably into its secret
ducting, both of my parents, a nurse, and the parents
of some kid with the forthright mishap
of a broken wrist (who were simply waiting around) all
ganged together in a choral demanding of *Why?* and not
just once, but with an annoying and increasingly fruitless
repetition.
                    I wouldn't say. I was too modest. It felt
unseemly to me, to reveal at this admittedly
awkward moment of tweezers and flashlight, how, although
indeed I'd undergone this temporary setback (as did
Edison, for example, who supposedly tried spinning
a newly grooved record around the inside of his mouth, to see
if his teeth would conduct the music directly
up his skull and into the brain . . . a most unlikely,
dead-end line of exploration, but evidently it needed
testing, to be eliminated) I'd been
in the rigorous process, admirably enough, of pioneering
the mapping-out of the human body's mysterious inner chancels
and circuitries by the introduction of tiny and assimilatable objects
(the pea was the first) . . . a process that still required fine-tuning
and yet was obviously bountiful in promise.
                                        Oh we're so clever,
oh we're so endlessly inquisitive and driven to tinker,
to theorize, to redo and adorn, to jigger zaps of electricity
into a dead frog's legs and zoom to the moon—the *moon!*—and
formulate grand cathedrals of numbers on our chalkboards
that encompass such angels as Gravity and Time.
Of course. We're cousin (to the *nth*, but still a cousin) to the apes
who think to poke their sticks inside the hills

—the little condominiums—the ants build, and then wait
to see those tastinesses obligingly skitter up.
                                        The entire
vast tree of our ancestry is shot through with the itchy juice
of dreaming of improvement. Velcro! Talkies! Twitter!
Salk vaccine! The tiny patented part that attaches
around that other part, here, on the gizmo: look at it
chutter along as smooth as molasses *now*!
                                        Yes, some
refinements to an earlier model are crackerjack ideas.
Whoever realized—*eureka*—that the razz-noise
she was puffing through a hollow bone could be improved
by diligently drilling four small holes into what became the world's
first flute . . . deserves an uncontestable A+.
But, I'm sorry, it's F for Christopher Smart,
industriously yanking away at the tails
of his "cat organ" which, as its name unashamedly indicates,
was cats trapped in the slats of a wooden contraption,
each supplying a note of the evening's rollicking
musical composition . . . even given three hundred years or more
of changing cultural sensibilities, something seems
amiss here. There are obvious highs (while I'm no fan
of warfare, still . . . how *cool* is the "invisibility cloak"
our physics wizardboys are researching for the military!)
and other ingenuities for which the word "low"
is inadequate (as one example, the catapulting
of flaming chickens over the enemy's ramparts) but,
no matter the results, the urge behind these
—our compulsion to rewrite what's come before, and
zing it zowier—is in us down to the cytoplasm,
unshakeably: we're whipped by psychic cilia
into frenzies of high-minded doctoring
(or "monkeying," as David Quammen writes—an unintentional joke—

"with his text": on Darwin's fussing
through six editions of *The Origin of the Species*).

As for the pea,
it had a future—thanks to Gregor Mendel,
that Austrian monk in his garden rows
conducting unmonkish study, probing
deeply into the proto-green, the microscopic generative green
inside the green pea, and returning with the principles
of heredity as a gift to the world.

He'd understand,
and Darwin understand, my parents' pride in their
collaborative effort at improving the human genome
—me. Their firstborn. Their Albie, destined
for a life of fulfillments immeasurably
beyond their own. And yet . . . in Immanuel Kipnis's office
that ruinous afternoon, they must have had their doubts
as, with a flourish Houdini would have appreciated,
the pea was extracted and held up for their stupefied inspection.
My younger sister, Livia, may be the proof of their growing need
to go back to the drawing board.

The universe
must look at us, at all of us, with similar conflictedness
of pride and disappointment. Part of nature
that we are, there is no end to our spinning wheels.
Stuff of the stars that we are, somebody's brain is aglow
all night in the lab, in quest of a cure
for cardiac blockage. Stuff of the stars that we are,
somebody is burning all night with the vision
of a better deep fat fryer: he can't stop,
it's in him, it churns in his heart.

Dentures

Upon his successfully completed solo flight to Paris, Charles Lindbergh
created for himself "fame on a scale and intensity unlike any experienced
by any human before. Tens of thousands of people rushed across the
airfield to Lindbergh's plane. 'It was like drowning in a human sea,' he
reported. On the morning after his arrival, cleaners gathered more than a
ton of lost property, including six sets of dentures."

—arranged from Bill Bryson's *One Summer*

The more—that's where our glory
and our sickest overweenings breed and drive us
like an engine: the more; our hunger for it; our need
to fill the zero-hole inside us with more
to metabolize, and then more.
                              One Buddhist precept
says "Whoever would gain blessings from a ritual prayer (*dharami*)
must write out seventy-five exact copies
and then place them in a pagoda": the empress Shotoku, deeply
thankful that her person had been spared from a contagion
of smallpox, thankful that her rule had survived
an eight-years-long rebellion, and (I'm guessing this)
feeling just a wee bit . . . empressy, ordered
one million copies, printed on strips of mulberry paper
eighteen inches long . . . perhaps (like many of us) she was drunk
one day on the bottomless abundance of the world and,
staring mesmerized by wildflowers riotously covering
the hills in their unending displays
of natural brocade, she grew inspired for her gratitude
to emulate the total more of the universe; or maybe
(again, like many of us) she simply felt a nothingness
inside, which is also ubiquitous through the universe, and thought to use
the absolute authority of her throne to feed it.
                                        To feed it,
desert saints have battled entire armies of devilspawn

that surrounded their comfortless sleeping mats
with stenches and clamors and bared phantasmal breasts
as orchestrated by the Ancient Evil himself; and, for the most
impressive entry in her filmography, the porn star Houston
serviced a line of 500 men in a row (assistants
attending her with bottles of spray-on lube);
                                   and Charles Lindbergh
flew 3,600 miles from Long Island to Paris, alone,
in a cloth-skinned plane without a window view
out the front, without a radio or a lifeboat,
with his logbook bobbing crazily on his knees and a flashlight
gripped between his teeth so he could try to scratch
his calculations into the log at night, and this
in a time when merely getting off the ground
was an achievement; he did it
casually, he did it as if he were born to it,
having spent his youth in barnstorm loop-de-loops, now
he was famished for more, and so he ate those thousands
of miles of ocean air, as Rosa Parks was famished
for justice and dignity and flew at these full-tilt
by sitting still. There are so many ways.
                                     Compounded
of examples, what I'm writing here is itself
one more example. The wife whose six biological children need
to be addended with four adopted more; her milquetoast husband, whose
addition of another babysitter to his list of diddled conquests
lifts it up now to a counterbalancing ten. We want more
Earth-like planets with water, we want more voter turnout,
more peace, more war, more highway miles per hour. Ihara Sakaku,
the 17th-century poet of Osaka, received the honorific nickname
"Twenty-thousand Old Master": in a marathon performance
he composed and recited 23,500 haiku

in continuous delivery: did each one feel like one more
tiny stepping-stone to the Hall of Immortal Grace?
                                        When
Charles Lindbergh landed triumphantly on the grassy field of Le Bourget,
the throng waxed out of control with wanting some portable
good-luck token of his more: they tattered fabric
off the body of the plane, and a man who was mistaken
for Lindbergh was carried around by the crowd and, at his rescue,
was "missing his coat, his belt, his necktie, one shoe,
and about half his shirt." Imagine the quieted
scene on that following morning, the cleaners puzzledly
goggling at the scattered debris, as if at scattered fossils on what
was once the ocean floor: umbrella fish; belt buckle trilobites;
and six pristine examples
of an early creature, all teeth, all chomp,
just waiting to evolve into us.

Our Place

Whatever it was we didn't hear—some pitch
the human ear can't catch—the dogs did,

and the night became their opera, scored for howling.
Or the bees: they maze through flowerscapes

the edges of the summer light make visible for them
(the way acoustic ricochet makes space

apparent to the bat) that we'd bump
headlong into or step from and plummet.

These platitudes about our place in the animal world
occasionally comfort me when I think how

my wife's head, after all this time, is really still
a capsule from another planet, sent to mine

with dreams inside, and algorithms, and sets
of assumptions, intended to test the limits

of my senses. Every morning there she is,
a mystery-aura'd visitor on whom the trees of the front yard

dapple the light: her breasts, her shoulder blades. I mean
the light we see by, that we call "the light"

although of course the other light, the greater light,
is wings on either side.

One of Them Speaks:

You said they turned you into a column of light
that traveled up itself, erasing itself in rising,
and so arrived on their ship. And then
a panel of "sensors" and "probers"
entering you—but these were also of light—
and pain, and the breaking of something even deeper
than intimacy; and then there was the feeling something higher than you
had lifted you to the warmth and whirr of its chest.
The Earth was so far below, and they were so "advanced,"
your old life seemed to be pelagic; and then
they dropped you back at our door,
as if you were the morning paper—it was that easy for them.
I'm not hurt that you took this adventure
without me, took it down to some important
subcutaneous place. But what hurts
is the way that you return there every night, your eyes
and your heart turned toward that wildness
when you were most alive. Or am I only talking of anybody
lost to an earlier time, and with a previous person, never having
fully traveled away from that psychoformative past?
—in which case, every marriage I know
is someone in bed and someone floating out of it
among the stars, though the body remains.
The body remains, but its force is journeying
somewhere else, and so, so far . . .
the way we think the dead do.

Novelist Russell Banks, on His Mentor the Novelist Nelson
Algren: "He took a lot of young writers literally under
his wing. . . ."

Which raises the question:
can a literal shelter be found
beneath a metaphorical wing?

Confusion
—or anyway, alternate states—abound
in classical images of certain seminal myths.
In one, the swan is nested on Leda's lap
no larger than a teddy bear. In one, it's the size
of a bull or larger (why not?—Zeus used bulls as well,
to make himself incarnate) and Leda
is nearly lost to view in that enormous flurry
of pinions and lust.

Frescoes,
tile mosaics, oil on canvas, engravings. . . .
One is brutal.
The clawed webs hold her immobile
and the beak has forcefully burrowed into her mouth,
as the great deep thrusts head home
between splayed-open thighs, and a look of mixed-together
terror and resignation opaques her eyes.

Another one
is transcendently lovely . . . gentle, even.
Twilight. Early spring.
A mutuality of desire blends the white down and her pale skin
into a single painted image of after-coupling satiation.
The setting is ferns and palm fronds, everything
green and yielding and lush.
Like Mary—a different tradition altogether, and yet

a similar circumstance—she's glowing now
with godhood. And—a metaphor himself—he lifts
one metaphorical wing above their heads
that, in this garden bower,
is literal in its attempt to make a sanctum for them,
for a while. It reminds me of the wedding canopy
Jews set up at their ceremonies, the *huppa*.
I even had one at mine.

Mélange

The village's sausage specialty
was pork and chicken ground
as fine as a mist—or sometimes
chicken and mollusc,
maybe beef and shad, or—
they could sometimes find a talon
or a beak in the mix,
like punctuation. And so
these were something like mythological creatures,
a griffin, a centaur:
more than one,
in one.
It reminds me of what I've read
about the shoddier mummifications
in ancient Egypt: occasional bones
of birds, of sows, of feral cats
were added in, to help out, clumsily, when
a human part went missing: presumably
sometimes someone woke up
in the Fields of Everlasting with an arm
and, on her other side, in an uneasy balance,
a wing. She might consider herself
a slightly third-rate version
of the gods—those lovely human bodies,
male and female both, but with the heads
of hawks or ibises or lions, with the aspect
of the ape, the hippopotamus, the scorpion.
And when I think, too,
of the many generations of consistency
with which that village served up
those mélange-ingredients sausages
at ceremonial feasts, I have to believe
they were intended—at least originally—

to be a reminder, a symbol, of how
the wedding bed is also the salty arithmetic
of $1 + 1 = 1$; how Jesus is
the great incinerating wrath of the tiger
and, equally, the mild
turned cheek of the lamb. If "sausage"
stands for "symbiosis," then it's everywhere
from our guts to our graves—bacteria
will vouch for that, ditto the maggot—although
my favorite example this week
is the umber and buff-tone Cypriot vase
from the 13th century B.C., with
(in simple but elegant silhouette)
"a bird removing a tick from a bull's neck";
charmingly, the bull inclines its head
in a bow, as you might for your barber or beautician,
to provide an easier access. Bull and tick,
then bull and bird—it's a *triangulated*
symbiosis, done up as a single,
sinuous, almost abstract design.
But Albert, it's not only beasts—for example,
wheat is alive. Well, yes; I've read a book
that basically posits wheat used us
—that *it* manipulated *us*—
into domesticating it, tending it
into a healthier thriving. Isn't the giant
plastic chicken holding a shock of wheat
in its humanish hands (and sometimes dancing)
on the roof of *Chicken-n-Biscuit Inn*
another example the villagers I began this with
would recognize? I'm not sure. And you,
—you, reading this—and me; another
example? What I *am* sure of,

having shared it with you, is how
there are mornings, wakings-up,
when a gossamer web of dream still clings
to your brain, still wants to claim you,
and you look down to the arms at your sides
or across your chest in a sad, confused
uncertainty . . . for a moment
you were sure you could fly.

I mistyped "Jump"

and so saw,
as if risen up from a kind of communityplasm,

how the rage my body shares with the rest of the species,
a blanketing crimson rage, a dagger-shape of rage,
the kind that seized control of Allie J
on finding her man in the back booth with Yolanda
and resulted in a bottle in her fist
and (from her man) a torn aorta
and (Yolanda) a muddle of teeth and blood on the floor

is also the rage—the same splenetic haze and dagger—
that drives the warriors, crazy for death,
with death in their hearts, with crazy in their hearts,
to the enemy village,
over the wall of thorns around its kraal,
half-a-planet away

from Bobby's Beer & Billiards on south Sixteenth.
Also, the chains of flowers the children sing their rhymes about
(and have for thousands of years)
in the village clearing saved for their play
are the very chains of flowers
the children are singing about in Chicago
and Tallahassee and Seattle, the flowers, the patterns,
that open unbidden in their minds
as they skip and sing and skim with their "Jung rope,"

as I typed it—which began all of this,
and ends it, and makes of these minds
a single collective.

Ecstasy!

—but not what you're thinking. Ecstasy originally: *ex*, "out of," +
histasthai, "to be standing": when some thunderbolt emotion
shatters you out of yourself. In ancient Greek calamities—say,
when Procne kills and dismembers her son, simmers
this chopmeat, serves it to her husband (the father)—suddenly
there's a snap of recognition so beyond the mind's ability
to accommodate, that a new—a second—mind is fissioned
out of the first: a fevered, monster mind, to meet
the monstrous situation. / There's a researcher with an archive
of thousands of photographs snapped at the pinpoint of disaster
—say, a red-scrolled roller coaster car
uncoupling, and a second, see-through rider is fissioned
out of the panicked corporeal one. It looks like a trick of the light
at first: if the light had a mouth, and was screaming.

———————

After eighteen hours of labor, Rebecca delivered twins
to the world on a rolled-out rug of silty uterine blood:
"At the final spasm, my consciousness floated above my body,"
meaning there was yet *another* umbilicus, a spectal rope
attaching her to her ecstasy-self, in that crowded room. / A hooker,
Ashlee tells me, does the same: divides in two, the personality
becoming housed in a cloud that floats above
the automatic writhing. / There were holy desert hermits
who would fast until their hunger was the size of a bean,
their sleep was only a crust of sleep. But for them,
this was joy. What you and I might find torturing,
they pushed to the next stage: mystical escape.
They exited out of the flesh, and into an exultation
only measurable by the wing-claps of angels.

———————

And isn't it similar (although I haven't kept current)
for mild-mannered Dr. Bruce Banner?—anger enough, and he
kafooms, uncontrollably, into The Hulk, a creature about the size
of a minivan (green), looking for someone to clobber
at the corner of Rage and Fury. / In the south of France in 1809,
a girl is brought to the village priest. Wait—make that
a "girl." She *looks* like a girl, though only walks
(adroitly) on all fours; she must be six and yet her only speech
is yelping. She was found in a cave, in her own shit
and the fresh shit of a wolf, and now this gentle man
must take her to his home and gently make her only one
of her two selves. "My child," he says—as if she were his daughter.
If a priest could have a daughter, if his daughter
opened jaws that howled unstoppably at the full of the moon.

———————

"It was the most powerful and important speech
heard in the Congress since it first convened. Recalling the moment
long afterward, [John] Adams would say he had been carried
out of himself, 'carried out in spirit,' as enthusiastic
preachers sometimes express themselves"—David McCullough. /
It's twilight in the village—it's a viscous mix of equal
day and night. The priest looks in at his difficult charge,
his squirming wolf/girl as she sleeps her inscrutable sleep
in the bed below a carven figure of the thorned and nailed
man/god on the wall. And though he looks long, and he isn't
short on pensive contemplation of these two
antipodean beings for whom he feels such affection,
neither the tragedy nor the glory of them—or of any of us—
gets clarified under his gentle, uncensorious stare.

———————

What he was, he was a "wanderer" [shaman initiate],
he walked alone in the forest, he spoke to invisible ones,
he fell to the ground and beat at his head, his eyes,
until he saw the far places. Many times, he did this.
And because of this he welcomed the gods. They accepted him,
they made him into a wolf, he fought like a wolf
—his food, his love, he took the way a wolf does.
When they were done and he was a person again, the gods
set his head on a flat rock, and from there he watched them
eat the flesh from his bones, he watched them from outside of his body
as they cleaned the bones, and then they restored the flesh
and then the head. Because of this, what he is, among us
he is a healer. His soul can travel up to the gods and bring back
"ancient rainbow" [healing powers]; *because of this we praise him.*

———————

Sometimes you drive at night, the houses left and right
no more than blurs upon the night, the stars a speeding surface
streaked unreadably—as if you're traveling up a vein
in an alien body. This is when you understand you're capable
of anything, some *you* of you could separate out, and be whatever
shape the night required. . . . / "Varro (116–27 B.C.) believed,
like most of his contemporaries, that bees could be
descended from bees *or* from rotting carcasses of oxen."
Maybe this is the poem that asks to be a rationale
for things I've done—for blots upon the rest
of who I am—that make me shameful. I did those things;
and I didn't. A small, released part of me did them:
a bee, that unlike the others was born of a rotting ox,
and flew directly away from the promise of light and honey.

These Risings Up. These Appearances.

It took a week for the lathe board on the floor
of the lake to be nudged aside by the bottom currents
enough:
          and then the body rose to the surface,
ballooned as it was with the gasses of decomposing.
The girl who wandered that shore that night
—her seven-year-old's understanding already
a jumble of fairy lore and magical occasions—saw
it happen, and for the rest of her life
remembers the wonder:
                a woman's face, ascended
through this placid water, exactly filling
—exactly completing—
the full face of the moon.

These risings up.
These appearances.

Palimpsest:
from the Greek *palimpsestos,*
"scraped again." Since parchment was expensive,
instead of merely discarding a once-used sheet,
it was scraped clean.
          But the ink used then,
an "iron gall ink," bonds chemically
with parchment—doesn't merely ride
the surface, but sinks into the fibers.
Keith Houston: "Many palimpsests
carry the shadows of their former texts";
though I would say "ghosts,"
sometimes eloquent ghosts, their spidery articulation
haunting the page,
          as when, from below

a medieval prayerbook's lustrously beetle-wing
blue-black ink, "two lost works by Archimedes"
declared themselves in 2011, evidently having
—as ghosts are said to do—unfinished business
here, among the living.

———————

In certain slants of light
sometimes, with certain paintings, you can see
a specter of the earlier face
—before the revision.
                        The earlier lover,
covered by the current.
                        The murderous regent
who was bodily dragged from his throne
to his death, and then (the artist
wasn't a fool) become the base for a portrait
of the murderous usurper: we can say that,
in a way, he was beheaded
twice.
        And here's the faintest tracery
of one of the vanquished, one of the endless, wan,
inconsequential poor, the neck
a wilting stem, the eyes downcast . . .
                                become
—a final version—the famous showcase oil
that the catalog titles *Defiance*.

Fossils: can we call these fossils?
Do any art historians call them fossils?

What the surgeons and nurses joked about
with a scathing merriment (yes:

it was you) while you
were 20,000 leagues below an ether sea
. . . it will come back, months or years,
but it will come back from its underconscious storage

as surely as trolley tracks in my childhood
that had been paved over
were known to surface, topping a bunched-up thrust
of gritty undersoil, and were the silvery
fossils of an earlier era
                              bright
amid the umber bricks.

———————

She was sleeping. He was awake,
beside her. All night, off and on, he watched
her face, that often wasn't the face
he knew and loved and argued with
and still loved. It was her, alright,
it was her. But . . .
a reorganized her, the features
gone mysterious. The deepest her,
unmoored
and, under the spell of the moon,
across vast distance,
visiting the upper world.

"Sometimes when Wordsworth was a child he had to reach out and touch a tree in order to reassure himself that he actually existed."

—Jonathan Bate

Surely this explains why we're needy for love.
Or, some of us, hate. In either case,

an other. By definition, we're
its other: and so this proves we're

really here. Our atoms, true,
are mostly emptiness, our "thoughts"

and "soul" are . . . try to weigh them,
or hold them up to a mirror. But the ball

returns on the racquet ball court,
the preacher's robust call receives

—creates—the congregation's counterbalancing
response: at which point, both

are confirmed. A friend of mine
confessed once—there was trust involved in this,

and also alcohol—that there was a time
years earlier, "a shaky, shaky time"

she said, when she would dial
strangers' phones at random,

not to prank, but just to have another
human voice be actual, and so prove

she was actual: "Annoyance worked for that
as well as empathy. That was many of me

ago." Why *shouldn't* we be this way,
if our gods are this way? They need to touch

our belief, to see that is has texture
and living sap, that it won't disappear,

and if it does *they'll* disappear.
They need to see that our faith is a tree.

A Standard Unit of Measurement

Lightning. Then, six heartbeats later,
its thunder. We say "thunder and lightning"
as if they were separate phenomena, but

they're one, of course, at two speeds.
It's the way our myths about Why Death
or Why Creation are really only stories

about a single state of existence
at two velocities. And in between the two:
six heartbeats. Lately, I find it everywhere.

The immediate glory (or pain) of love.
        [six heartbeats]
    Then our song about it.

GPS

G. K. Chesterton would be so lost in thought, that he'd
forget his surroundings. One time, during a lecture
tour, he sent Frances a telegram: "Am in Birmingham.
Where ought I be?"

—Bill Peschel

Alexander van Humboldt (1770–1859), early nineteenth-century
Renaissance man (naturalist, cartographer, author, engineer,
and—not least—explorer) whose life and works, whose
unprecedented epic travel, inspired Darwin and Goethe among
a host of others, and who pioneered an ecological vision
of the connectedness of all life on our planet.

1.

Dora's has the velvety stroke-my-fur-please
purr of a would-be lover offering pleasure
and grapes and a lowball of sloe gin; Sandra's
slambangs-out instructions in the tones of a robot nun
demanding obedience. What all of them do is parcel out
the planet in disturbingly insulting, tiny
increments. *Go . . . to the end . . .*
of your own front porch . . . walk down . . . turn left . . .
as if the adventure of being alive required
a user's manual that's sized to human infancy.
Well, baby steps
is where we begin; and baby steps
we continue to take, compared to the immeasurable
universe we're traveling.

2.

The space ship zooms up, every second
farther apart from the capable wonks
of Ground Control, with their fidgety dials,
subtly blipping monitor screens, and other superduper
digital links by which they think of the ship
as a flown kite. But the genius of the geese
is, ground control is *with* them, *in* them,
born in the genome, smaller—electronmicroscopically
smaller—than even the two-inch sextant
(it was called a "snuffbox sextant") Humboldt
brought along in 1799, on a Spanish frigate,
to South America's unknown (well, unknown
to Europeans) swamps and highest peaks: a journey
of 6,4443 miles. Every second, farther.

3.

What's a star, if not a local idiom
of the über-language "Sky"
—itself a construct we create
to manage (so as not to descend
into madness) "Void" and "Infinity." For Raoul
it was packaged almost impossibly neatly: her name
was Starr. Her charms became a kind of radiant beacon
for his love. She moved to Santa Fe:
he moved to Santa Fe. She moved to Rome:
he moved to Rome. *Ms. Lodestone*—that's
the name we gave her; and the less charitable,
Ms. Lighthouse to Hell. And when she moved
for two years off the map, off the grid: he disappeared
as if the ground had swallowed him up whole.

4.

The south-pointing fish: a lovely name,
"the first unmistakable mention
of a compass," 1044 A.D. in a Chinese handbook
on military technology. It was indeed a pointer
of magnetized iron, fish-shaped, floating in a bowl,
the rim of which was inscribed with the four directions.
Fish: one thinks of the salmon's faultless
homing-in to home. Or an eel's ocean-wide migration
as finely tuned as if it were threading a needle.
Now, for us, it's all computerized. More simply,
Doctor Dolittle, when he's itching to go on a voyage,
"would take the atlas and open it with my eyes shut."
Wherever his pencil touches down . . . that's the X,
"The rules of the game say we've got to [go]."

5.

Humboldt's heroic odyssey of scientific exploration
and ceaseless, scrupulous measurement . . . we revel in
its dramatic tableaux: determining the voltage
of the electric eel *by gripping it*, repeatedly,
over a day; the adventures of entering the guano caves,
and of the solar eclipse; 600 new species identified;
climbing the volcano Chimborazo, to 19,286 feet
("higher than anybody had ever been, even in a balloon")
on ridges sometimes no wider than eight or nine inches.
But let's take a minute to recognize the workaday
fold-up sextant and its kindred packed in his travel bags:
tacks in the world's four corners that kept
the cosmos he loved with such ardor
from drifting off into "Void" and "Infinity."

6.

Two years later Raoul returned. And Starr?
"Pills, man. I was there when they pumped
her stomach" [then tears, then shivering as if
his bones were being shook like back-alley dice]
"and a mess came out, but not in time."
For months he wanted to die too, and our own lives
(all of his friends chipped in) had to die at the edges
a little, taking turns in keeping watch over him.
One night he had to be tied to a chair,
to keep him from a knife or a blind-drunk
after-midnight ride down the canyons.
Santa Fe. Rome. Madrid. Miami.
And now he wanted to follow her a final time,
over a final line, filings to a magnet.

7.

Back then, when I was twelve, the maps were paper
and if your journey was far your map was fat
and pleated, sometimes it felt it was as pleated
as an accordion. I can picture my father
driving, and my mother the navigator attempting
to read those indications of roads and rivers
like a seer bent to the veins of a slaughtered fowl.
Sometimes they'd argue: Left! NO, RIGHT!
Sometimes we'd arrive and it felt destined.
And I remember—because it happens at twelve—undoing
a *Playboy* centerfold: it too was a territory ahead,
of mystery and beckon. Thoreau: "I believe that there is a subtle
magnetism in Nature, which, if we unconsciously
yield to it, will direct us aright."

8.

Those geese from section 2?—have landed
here, in 8, for the night: a lengthy journey, but
their bodies read the map of sun and magnetism
as deftly as *you're* reading *this*. / The bee
is ably instructed by its hive-mate bees, whose bottom-wagging
"coordinates dance" is as meaningful as Boy Scout signals
bark-stripped into trees. Sweetness guides them. Light
beyond our spectrum channels them like traffic cones.
/ Butterfly migration. Bison migration. / Dime-turn
aerial sweeps of the dusk that bats conduct
by sound. / The lemmings know, deep-printed
in the know-part of their brain, and the unerring
one-way pilgrimage begins. / And Dora's strap-around
ankle chip that announces how many steps.

9.

Once I had a drink with a friend of Starr's.
His version wasn't Raoul the moth
forever approaching Starr the dangerous flame.
His version: Raoul the stalker, mad, obsessed,
"plain creepy"; there was an implication
her pills were a response to his relentlessness. Well . . .
the Polynesian "hand map," to my own unknowing eyes,
looks like a child's game, a simple flattened-down
catscradle of crosshatched sticks, but it represented
ocean currents well enough for thousand-mile voyages
on balsa rafts; and then there's Sandra's robot nun
conversing with some satellite . . . *Turn right in one half-mile.* . . .
Versions. Versions. Every traveler on this Earth
is traveling a different Earth.

10.

We used to call it "the ship of state," the metaphor
being a sailing vessel, a frigate let's say,
fully-masted and under robust sail, laden
with bounty, breasting the seas with a proud
assurance, and proud of its flag, and welcome,
aloha, in any port of call. But now
on grayer days I suspect that my country
has lost its way. I feel that I'm,
we're, all of us, on a voyage without
direction, the compass beyond repair.
In camp A, all of us feel it. Everybody
in camp Z too. And yet we mean opposing things
by that. Every culture sailing on this Earth
is sailing a different Earth.

11.

The children are grown and gone, and I'm retired,
and I'm lost, I have no Pole Star anymore.
Are you in a place called "home," but a stranger there?
I'm "home," but I'm a stranger to myself.
My [ ] husband [ ] wife [ ] God [ ] body
has changed over time, and I'm unmoored, I'm lost,
without an astrolabe. *Are you without an astrolabe?*
Yes, nothing interior lines up anymore with the world outside.
     Nicholas Carr (in his book *The Glass Cockpit*) says
     the ubiquitous GPS toolkit "end[s] up isolating us
     from the environment," and erodes our autonomy.
     "Paper maps teach us how to think about space."
Are you lost in a landscape you once used to know?
Yes, I'm lost in a landscape I once used to know.

12.

Everybody, in unison:
Universe, please guide me, guide me benevolently;
if not, please let me guide myself by the light
of an interior Beatrice atom or a Virgil atom;
Dante relied on their global (and fabled after-global) positioning
for his difficult trail, let me be found worthy
of them; and of an interior atom of quick, wisecracking
taxi dispatcher straight from a 1940s screwball movie;
Universe, let me point like a setter, swivel true
like a weathervane, let me heed the clarion call
to an end: a good end. Because he carried his instruments
over icy scarps and through the desert wastelands
faithfully, position in me an atom that the Periodic Table
labels Humboldtsextant: *tiny, unfailing, sufficient unto my life.*

Amen.

Stories

That piercing shriek of Fay Wray's in the center
of King Kong's palm is as startlingly raw
as if a stigmata hole has opened up. Its power
is inherited from just a flicker of movie history
earlier, when genius is in silence

turning eloquent . . . transforming lack
to bounty. Buster Keaton,
Chaplin, Lillian Gish . . . it's everything
we *can't* hear that we hear from them
most loudly. The Louis Simpson poem

about the Allied prisoner of war who keeps himself sane
by drawing a piano keyboard and practicing
a music only he can hear. And somewhere
a woman is screaming—right now, a woman alone
in her bed is sitting up and screaming

and screaming. I don't know who, or where, but there's never
a moment without this somewhere-woman,
and she's screaming in the purest way: it doesn't require
our ears. Archeologists have discovered a well
in an ancient desert city, carved on its inside

all the way down to what was once water level.
"We can't translate the writing or know
its purpose. Probably there are other such wells,
as yet undiscovered." The whole night: listen:
stone throats full of haunting, inaudible stories.

ACKNOWLEDGMENTS

Some poems in this book have appeared (occasionally in an earlier version) in the following journals, the editors of which I thank not only for their generosity to me, but for continuing to maintain, issue after issue, for all of us, honorable standards (and consistent reading pleasure) in the current publishing world:

American Poetry Review, Conduit, December, Georgia Review, Gettysburg Review, Green Mountains Review, I-70, New Letters, Southern Review, 32 Poems. Special thanks to editors Stephen Corey, Mark Drew, Christie Hodgen, Gianna Jacobson, Herb Leibowitz, and Bob Stewart for their spot-on taste and helpful suggestions.

And for various kinds of aid and cheerleading, my gratitude goes out to Michele Battiste, Alice Friman, Natalie Garyet, Christopher Howell, Joey Lemon, Toni Loeffler, Rick Mulkey, and Wayne Zade—mensches all. Ed Ochester's editorial acumen, of course, hovers above a breathtakingly enormous percentage of the best of contemporary American poetry.

None of these poems was written, researched, or submitted using computer technology; a tip o' the hat to the United States Postal Service and mail carrier Nancy.